ANIMAL LIFE CYCLES

Ladybug

by Elizabeth Neuenfeldt

BELLWETHER MEDIA • MINNEAPOLIS, MN

Blastoff! Readers are carefully developed by literacy experts to build reading stamina and move students toward fluency by combining standards-based content with developmentally appropriate text.

Level 1 provides the most support through repetition of high-frequency words, light text, predictable sentence patterns, and strong visual support.

Level 2 offers early readers a bit more challenge through varied sentences, increased text load, and text-supportive special features.

Level 3 advances early-fluent readers toward fluency through increased text load, less reliance on photos, advancing concepts, longer sentences, and more complex special features.

★ **Blastoff! Universe**

Reading Level

Grade
K

Grades
1–3

Grade
4

This edition first published in 2021 by Bellwether Media, Inc.

No part of this publication may be reproduced in whole or in part without written permission of the publisher. For information regarding permission, write to Bellwether Media, Inc., Attention: Permissions Department, 6012 Blue Circle Drive, Minnetonka, MN 55343.

Library of Congress Cataloging-in-Publication Data

Names: Neuenfeldt, Elizabeth, author.
Title: Ladybug / by Elizabeth Neuenfeldt.
Description: Minneapolis, MN : Bellwether Media, 2021. | Series: Blastoff! readers: Animal life cycles | Includes bibliographical references and index. | Audience: Ages 5-8 | Audience: Grades K-1 | Summary: "Relevant images match informative text in this introduction to the life cycle of a ladybug. Intended for students in kindergarten through third grade"-- Provided by publisher.
Identifiers: LCCN 2020036807 (print) | LCCN 2020036808 (ebook) | ISBN 9781644874103 (library binding) | ISBN 9781648340871 (ebook)
Subjects: LCSH: Ladybugs--Life cycles--Juvenile literature.
Classification: LCC QL596.C65 N48 2021 (print) | LCC QL596.C65 (ebook) | DDC 595.76/9156--dc23
LC record available at https://lccn.loc.gov/2020036807
LC ebook record available at https://lccn.loc.gov/2020036808

Editor: Betsy Rathburn   Designer: Jeffrey Kollock

Printed in the United States of America, North Mankato, MN.

Table of Contents

What Are Ladybugs?

Ladybugs are a type of **beetle**. These **insects** can live almost anywhere in the world!

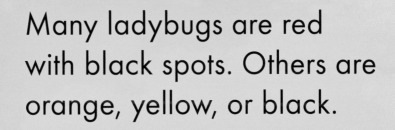

Many ladybugs are red
with black spots. Others are
orange, yellow, or black.

Life Cycle of a Ladybug

The ladybug life cycle is called **metamorphosis**. It begins in spring.

Females lay egg **clusters** on the undersides of leaves. Clusters may have up to 50 eggs!

eggs

egg
cluster

Next, ladybugs leave to lay more eggs. They lay hundreds of eggs a year!

hatching

The eggs begin to **hatch**
within 10 days.

When eggs hatch, **larvae** come out. Ladybug larvae have six legs and dark, spiky bodies.

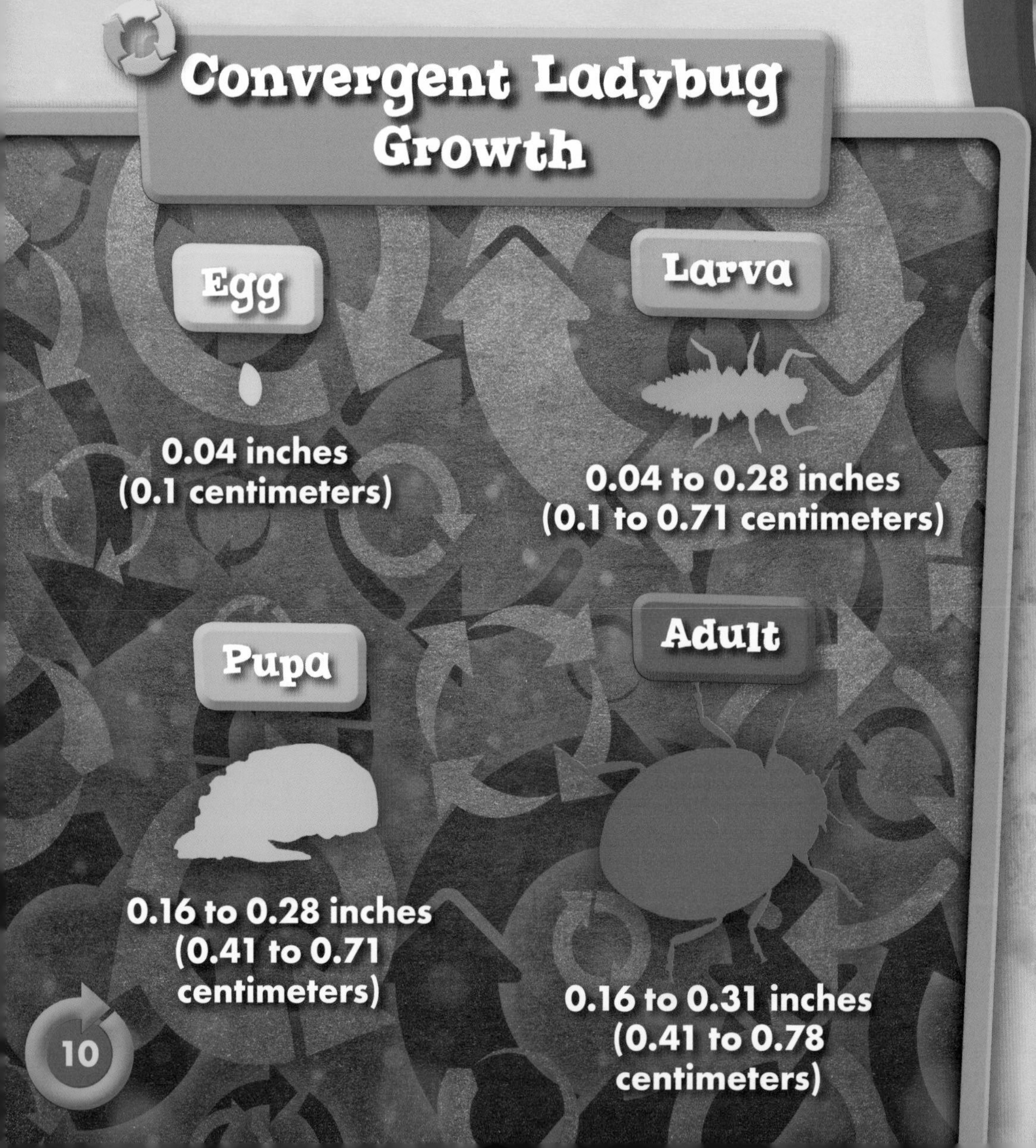

Convergent Ladybug Growth

Egg

0.04 inches
(0.1 centimeters)

Larva

0.04 to 0.28 inches
(0.1 to 0.71 centimeters)

Pupa

0.16 to 0.28 inches
(0.41 to 0.71
centimeters)

Adult

0.16 to 0.31 inches
(0.41 to 0.78
centimeters)

larva

The tiny larvae are less than
1 inch (2.5 centimeters) long.

aphids

molting

Ladybug larvae eat a lot of **aphids**! Larvae store **nutrients** from aphids in their bodies.

As larvae grow, they must **molt**. This makes more room for their growing bodies.

Ladybug Diet

Larva

aphids

Pupa

stored nutrients

Adult

aphids

13

About one month later, larvae attach their bellies to leaves. They form curved **cocoons**.

The larvae are now **pupae**.

cocoon

pupa

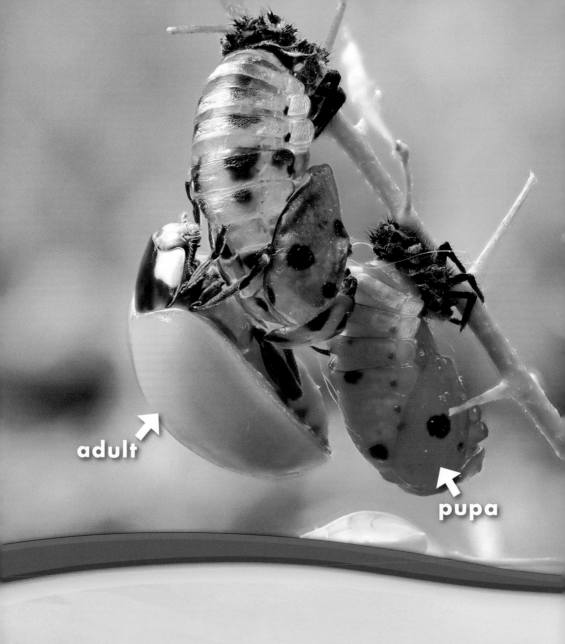

adult

pupa

Inside their cocoons, pupae feed on stored nutrients.

Growing Up: Convergent Ladybug

Egg		2 to 5 days
Larva		around 21 days
Pupa		up to 15 days
Adult		a few months

They stay in their cocoons for up to 15 days. Then adult ladybugs chew their way out!

Adult ladybugs are up to 0.4 inches
(1 centimeter) long. Most eat aphids.
Some eat **fungi**!

Ladybugs mostly live alone. But they sleep in groups during winter.

When spring returns, ladybugs **mate**. Soon, the ladybug life cycle begins again!

Life Cycle of a Ladybug

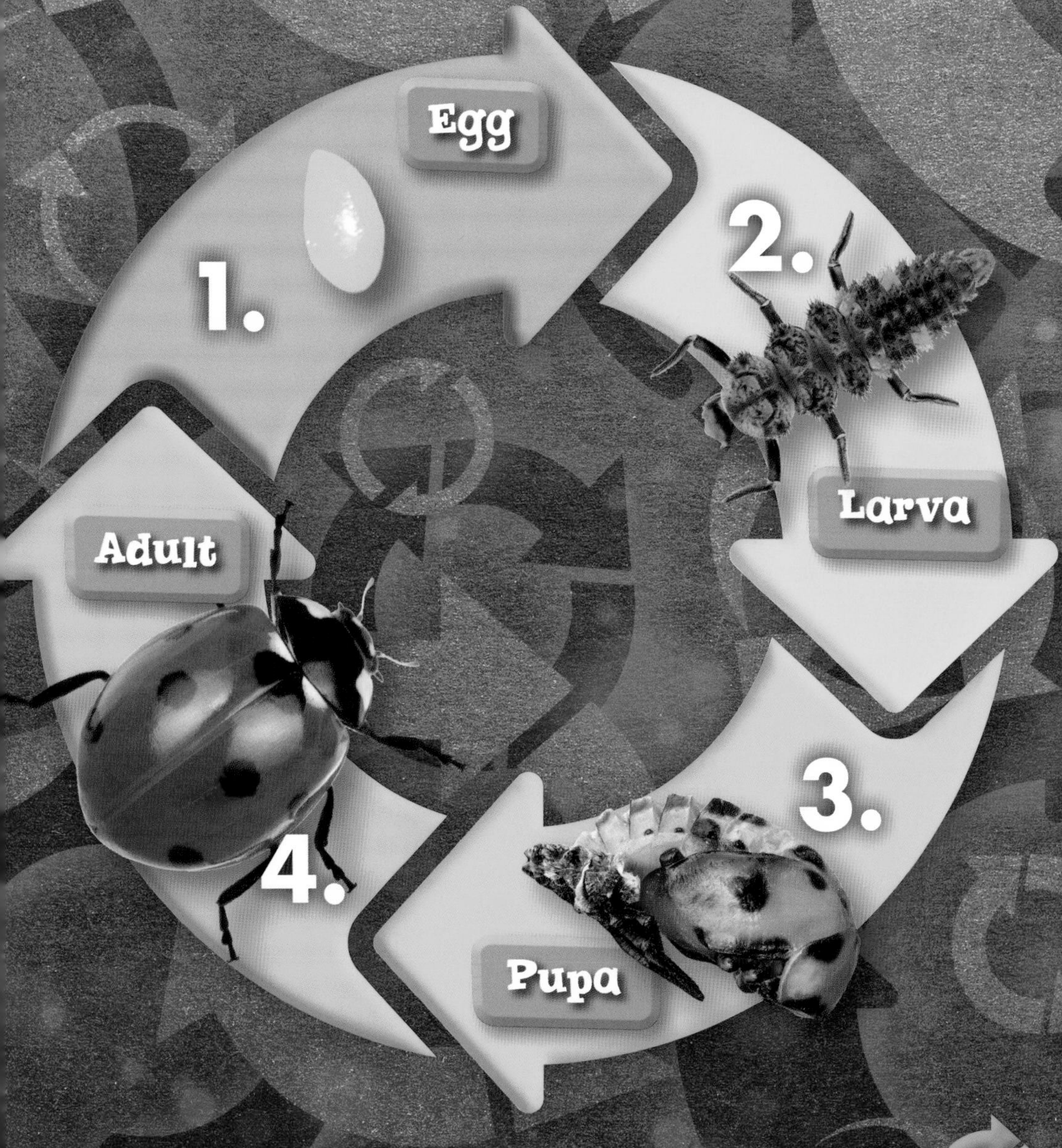

1. Egg

2. Larva

3. Pupa

4. Adult

21

Glossary

aphids—small insects that eat plants

beetle—a type of insect with four wings where the outer wings cover the others when the wings are folded

clusters—groups

cocoons—hard coverings in which insect pupae turn into adults

fungi—living things that are neither plants nor animals; mushrooms and molds are types of fungi.

hatch—to break out of an egg

insects—small animals with six legs and bodies divided into three parts

larvae—young insects that break out of eggs and look like small worms

mate—to join together to make young

metamorphosis—a big change in how some animals look and act, usually related to growing

molt—to shed skin so that new skin can grow

nutrients—substances that living things need to live and grow

pupae—young insects that create cocoons in which to change into their adult forms

To Learn More

AT THE LIBRARY

Kenney, Karen Latchana. *Life Cycle of a Ladybug.*
Minneapolis, Minn.: Jump! Inc., 2019.

Owings, Lisa. *From Egg to Ladybug.* Minneapolis,
Minn.: Lerner Publications, 2017.

Shea, Therese M. *Ladybugs Up Close.* New York,
N.Y.: PowerKids Press, 2020.

ON THE WEB

FACTSURFER

Factsurfer.com gives you
a safe, fun way to find
more information.

1. Go to www.factsurfer.com.

2. Enter "ladybug" into the search box
   and click 🔍.

3. Select your book cover to see a list
   of related content.

Index

The images in this book are reproduced through the courtesy of: Achkin, front cover, p. 1; Serg64, p. 3; InsectWorld, pp. 4, 5; L-N, p. 5; SweetCrisis, p. 6; lior2, pp. 6, 7; Jorge Abel Photography, pp. 8, 9; Andia/ Alamy, p. 9; sophiecat, pp. 10, 11; Catherine Eckert, pp. 12, 13; Dr.MYM, p. 12 (molting); Vera Larina, p. 13 (aphids); AC Rider, p. 13 (stored nutrients); zaidi razak, p. 14; Eduardo Estellez, pp. 14, 15; aaltair, pp. 16, 17; PictureDesignSwiss, pp. 18, 19; Rose Ludwig, p. 19; Room 76, p. 20; Andi111, p. 21 (egg); Anton Kozyrev, p. 21 (larva); ozgur kerem bulur, p. 21 (pupae); irin-k, p. 21 (adult); PHOTO FUN, p. 23.